Wealth Of Nations

Egypt

Cath Senker

HODDER
Wayland

an imprint of Hodder Children's Books

Wealth Of Nations series includes:

Brazil	India
China	Malaysia
Egypt	Vietnam

Cover: Main photo: The Mohammed Ali Mosque in Cairo. Inset: A boy in a market in Saqqara.

Title page: Women in their kitchen area in southern Egypt.

Contents page: A camel market in Cairo.

Egypt is a simplified and updated version of the title *Egypt* in Hodder Wayland's *Economically Developing Countries* series.

Text copyright © 2001 Hodder Wayland
Volume copyright © 2001 Hodder Wayland

Editor: Polly Goodman
Language consultant: Norah Granger, Senior Lecturer in Education Studies,
Department of Education, University of Brighton.

First published in Great Britain in 1995 by Wayland Publishers Ltd. This edition updated
and published in 2001 by Hodder Wayland, an imprint of Hodder Children's Books.

British Library Cataloguing in Publication Data
Senker, Cath
   Egypt. – (Wealth of Nations)
   1. Egypt – Economic conditions – 1952 – Juvenile literature
   2. Egypt – Social conditions – 1952 – Juvenile literature
   3. Egypt – Geography – Juvenile literature
   I. Title
   962' 055

ISBN 0 7502 3532 2

Printed and bound by G. Canale & C.S.p.A., Turin, Italy.

Hodder Children's Books
A division of Hodder Headline Limited
338 Euston Road, London NW1 3BH

Picture acknowledgements
All photographs are by James H. Morris, except: Associated Press 32 (top), 35; Camera Press 32 (bottom); Eye Ubiquitous *Cover, inset* (Julia Waterlow); *Cover, main* (Simon Harris); Topham Picture Source 5 (bottom), 34; Wayland Picture Library 10, 31 (Julia Waterlow). Artwork by Hardlines.

CONTENTS

INTRODUCTION

Egypt is one of the oldest places where people have lived. There has been civilization along the River Nile for more than 5,000 years.

Egypt is a country full of contrasts. Most of the land is a huge, empty desert, where only a few people can make a living. The bustling, noisy cities, with their endless traffic jams, are home to nearly half the population. Other people live on tiny farms in villages along the River Nile.

A street market in Cairo. ▼

EGYPT'S NAME

The ancient Egyptians called the country *Het-ka-ptah*. When the Greeks arrived, they changed it to *Ai-gy-ptious*, which is where the English word 'Egypt' came from.

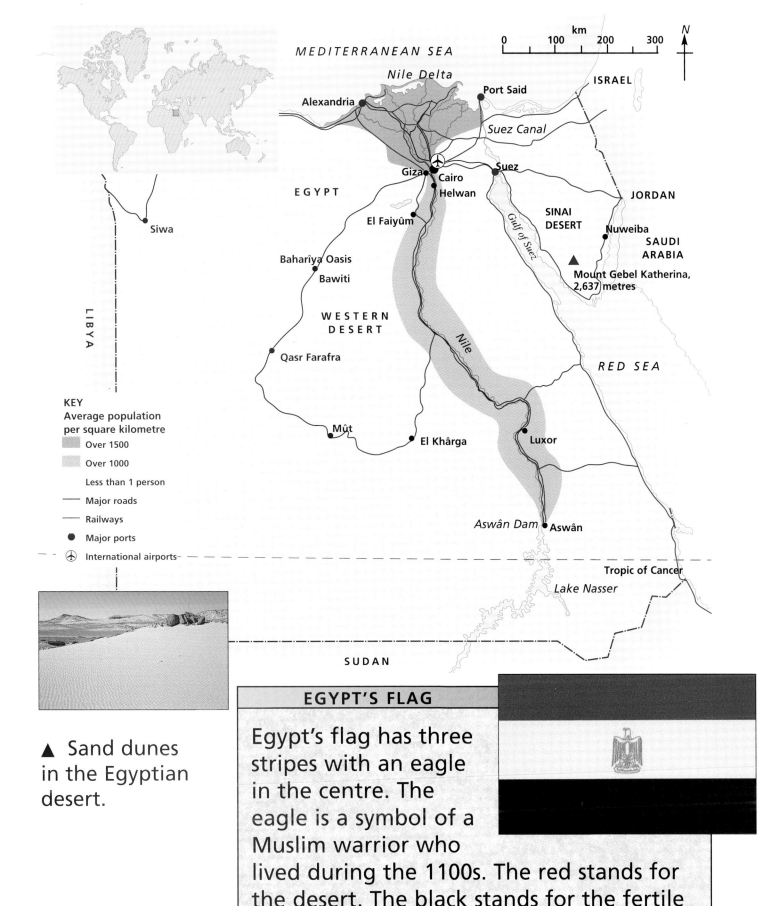

km
0   100   200   300

N

MEDITERRANEAN SEA

Nile Delta

Port Said

ISRAEL

Alexandria

Suez Canal

Giza

Suez

EGYPT

Cairo
Helwan

JORDAN

SINAI
DESERT

El Faiyûm

Gulf of Suez

Nuweiba

SAUDI
ARABIA

Baharîya Oasis

Bawiti

▲ Mount Gebel Katherina,
2,637 metres

WESTERN
DESERT

Nile

RED SEA

LIBYA

Siwa

Qasr Farafra

Mût

El Khârga

Luxor

KEY
Average population
per square kilometre

Over 1500

Over 1000

Less than 1 person

Major roads

Railways

Major ports

International airports

Aswân Dam ● Aswân

Tropic of Cancer

Lake Nasser

SUDAN

▲ Sand dunes
in the Egyptian
desert.

EGYPT'S FLAG

Egypt's flag has three stripes with an eagle in the centre. The eagle is a symbol of a Muslim warrior who lived during the 1100s. The red stands for the desert. The black stands for the fertile Nile valley and delta.

RICH AND POOR

Egypt is rich in natural resources. Yet it faces many problems. The population is growing fast. In 2000, 39 per cent of Egyptians were children under 15 years old. Many people are poor and it is hard for them to make enough money to look after their families.

People living in the desert. ▼

▼ A homeless person in Cairo.

EGYPT FACTS	
Population:	68 million
Area:	1,001,449 square kilometres
Capital city:	Cairo
Language:	Arabic
Main religion:	Islam

LAND AND CLIMATE

Egypt's natural features. ▼

Egypt is in the north-east of Africa. The Mediterranean Sea is to the north and the Red Sea is to the east.

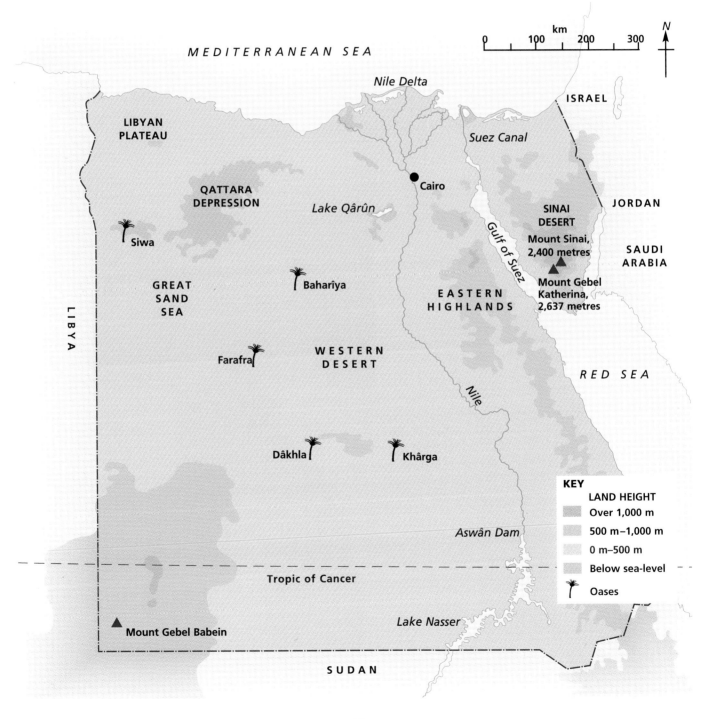

MEDITERRANEAN SEA

km
0   100   200   300

N

Nile Delta

ISRAEL

LIBYAN
PLATEAU

Suez Canal

QATTARA
DEPRESSION

Cairo

Lake Qârûn

SINAI
DESERT

JORDAN

Siwa

Mount Sinai,
2,400 metres

SAUDI
ARABIA

GREAT
SAND
SEA

Bahariya

EASTERN
HIGHLANDS

Mount Gebel
Katherina,
2,637 metres

L I B Y A

Farafra

WESTERN
DESERT

Gulf of Suez

Nile

R E D   S E A

Dâkhla

Khârga

KEY

LAND HEIGHT

Over 1,000 m

500 m–1,000 m

0 m–500 m

Below sea-level

Oases

Aswân Dam

Tropic of Cancer

Mount Gebel Babein

Lake Nasser

S U D A N

LANDSCAPE

Egypt is a large country, but most of it is desert. The desert areas are called the 'red lands' because of the colour of the sand and rocks there. The Western Desert has vast areas of sand dunes. But most of the desert is covered with gravel rather than sand.

The Sinai juts out into the Red Sea. The Sinai is a dramatic area of mountains, where the highest mountain in Egypt is found.

'We have always lived in the desert. More and more of us work with tourists now to make money.' – Mohammed, a Bedouin man from the Eastern Highlands

Highest point:	Mount Gebel Katherina, 2,637 metres above sea-level
Lowest point:	Qattâra Depression, 133 metres below sea-level.
Hottest place:	Aswân (average 40 °C)

A village in the middle of desert plains. ▼

◄ A Bedouin man from the Eastern Highlands.

8

◀ Feluccas are still used to travel on the River Nile.

RIVER NILE

Running through the deserts is the River Nile. From Lake Nasser in Sudan, the Nile flows towards the Mediterranean Sea, about 1,600 kilometres further north. Beside the river is the flood plain. This thin stretch of land is called the 'black land', because of its rich, dark soils.

After Cairo, the Nile divides into a delta, where it fans out into several channels. The Nile Delta is one of the largest deltas in the world. It is 250 kilometres wide when it reaches the Mediterranean Sea. Between the river channels, the fertile soil is planted with food crops.

In 1857, two Englishmen called Richard Burton and John Speke set off in search of the source of the River Nile. Burton got malaria and became very ill, so Speke carried on without him.

Speke discovered that the source was at Lake Victoria, but Burton did not believe him. Unfortunately, Speke died in a hunting accident before he could convince Burton that he was right.

This map of the River Nile was drawn in the second century by Ptolemy, an ancient Greek astronomer.▼

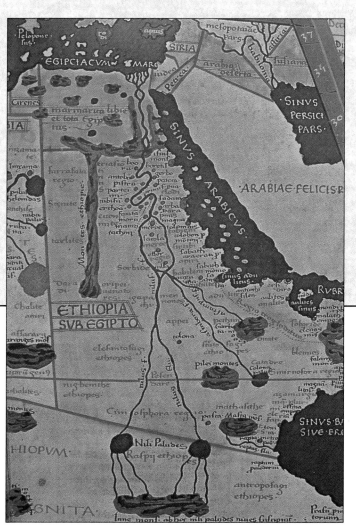

FLOODS

In the past, the River Nile used to flood each year. The floods spread silt and water beside the river, over land called the flood plain. Farmers planted their crops in the rich, damp soil. The Nile flood plain is one of the most fertile farming areas in the world.

Since the Aswân Dam was built in 1970, the River Nile no longer floods each year.

OASES

Across the vast stretches of desert, in some places an oasis appears. At an oasis, water can be pumped from underground and used to water crops. Many people live near oases, such as Baharîya and Siwa. They farm the fertile land.

▲ A farmer at an oasis.

HOW AN OASIS IS FORMED

When rain falls, water travels underground through porous rock. Where the rock is close to the surface, wells can be dug.

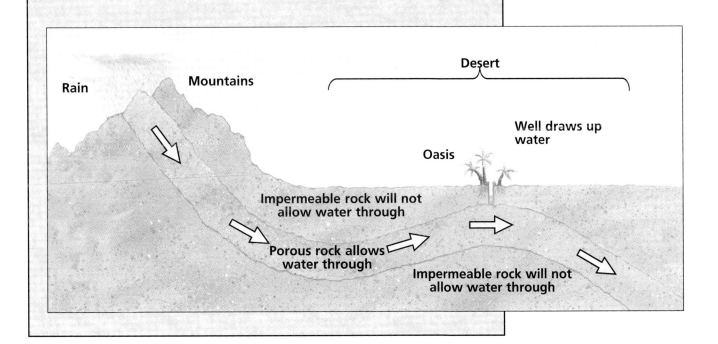

This canal gets its water from the River Nile. The precious water is used for crops. ▶

THE KHAMSIN

The khamsin is a hot, dry wind that sometimes blows from the desert in April. When the khamsin blows, the temperature can rise by up to 20 °C in a few hours. It is so fierce that it can blast paint from cars and destroy crops.

Sometimes the dust from the khamsin is carried so high that it blows to countries thousands of kilometres from Egypt.

CLIMATE

Egypt is in one of the hottest and driest countries in the world. There is very little rain. Even on the Mediterranean coast, where most of the rain falls, there is only about 200 millimetres of rain per year. This is a quarter of the world average.

Further south there is even less rain. In Aswân, there is only about 1 millimetre of rain per year! It is very hot, too. Temperatures of 42 °C are normal here.

THE PEOPLE OF EGYPT

A tomb painting showing daily life in Egypt over 2,000 years ago. ▼

▲ A colourful market in Cairo today.

Many thousands of years ago, North Africa was green and fertile. Then, between 10,000 and 20,000 years ago, the climate changed. The fertile plains turned to desert. So people moved to the rivers, especially the Nile in Egypt. They began to group together, hunting and gathering their food.

Around 7,000 years ago, people from Arabia and Asia brought farming skills to ancient Egypt. Farming began on the fertile land by the Nile, and the ancient Egyptian civilization grew. Egyptians learned to bake bread and brew beer. They built magnificent pyramids and temples.

STAR WORSHIP

Stars were important in the religion of the ancient Egyptians. They used detailed star maps to guide people at important times in their life, such as at their birth, coming of age and death.

The pyramids of Giza were placed so that each pyramid stood for a star in the Orion constellation (a group of stars).

A Nubian couple in southern Egypt. ▶

Some Bedouin people, like this man, still wander the deserts. Others have settled in towns. ▼

◀ The pyramids of Giza were built about 4,500 years ago.

MIXED PEOPLE

The ancient Egyptian civilization began to break up about 3,000 years ago. One after the other, Ethiopia, Persia, Greece, Rome, Arabia, Turkey and Britain ruled Egypt.

So Egyptians today are a mixed people. Their closest links are with the Middle East, and the main language is Arabic. In the north, especially in Alexandria, there is more of a European feel. In the south, where the Nubians live, it is more African.

'The Qur'an tells us how we should live our lives. I pray five times every day.' – Sherif, a Muslim man.

RELIGION	
Muslim	89%
Christian	10%
Others	1%

RELIGION

Most Egyptians are Muslims. The Islamic faith is based on a holy book, called the Qur'an. It is believed to be the words of God, as written down by the prophet Muhammad.

The Qur'an says that women should cover themselves. In Egypt, many women wear long gowns, headscarves and veils.

▲ Muslims praying in a mosque in Cairo.

▲ Muslims praying in Egypt. They always face east, towards Mecca in Saudi Arabia.

PRAYER

Muslims pray five times a day. A man called a muezzin sings out from every mosque to let people know when it is time to pray. Wherever they are, Muslims stop what they are doing. They lay down a small carpet facing the holy city of Mecca. Kneeling on the carpet, they say their prayers.

THE NUBIANS

Since ancient times, Nubian people have lived in the south of Egypt and the north of Sudan. They have lived separately from other people for thousands of years, so they have their own culture and language.

Nubians are a proud people. They are seen as the most gentle and peace-loving of Egyptians. Until recently, they lived a quiet, relaxed life in villages. Their large, mudbrick houses were always freshly painted. Nubians lived by herding animals and growing crops using simple methods.

▲ Few Nubians still live a traditional life.

But in 1970, their peaceful lives were ruined by the building of the Aswân Dam. Lake Nasser, which was created behind the dam, covered most of their land. Most Nubians had to leave their homes and move to new settlements built by the government.

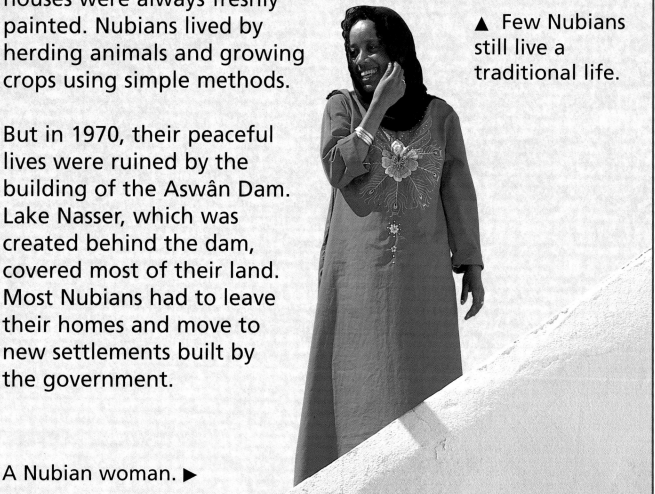

A Nubian woman. ▶

IN THE CITY

◀ Cairo at night. By 2015, the population will probably reach 13.8 million.

Egypt used to be a country of villagers farming by the Nile. Now, 43 per cent of the people live in cities. Cairo is Egypt's capital city and the largest city in Africa. It is a giant bustling city where 10.6 million people live and work.

EARTHQUAKE!

On 12 October 1992, an earthquake measuring 5.9 on the Richter scale shook Cairo. Although it was not a strong earthquake, 600 people were killed and 10,000 injured. This was because the buildings in the slum areas were poorly built so they collapsed easily, crushing the people inside.

Most people who come to Cairo for the first time are amazed at the traffic, the din of hooting cars, and the people filling the streets day and night. The city has a feeling of great excitement.

OLD AND NEW

Cairo is a fascinating mix of old and new. In the 1960s, thousands of modern blocks of flats were built. But among them are ancient mosques. Many are over 1,000 years old.

RICH AND POOR

There is also a big difference between rich and poor in Cairo. There are luxury hotels and large homes with servants for super-rich Egyptians. But there are not enough jobs, houses or schools for many of the people who move to the city from the countryside.

▼ Alexandria is Egypt's second-largest city.

In poor areas of the city, such as Old Cairo, large families are squashed into tiny one-room flats. Often they have no running water. Some people are so poor that they make their living selling goods they find in rubbish heaps.

Housing in a poor part of Cairo. ▶

CITY OF THE DEAD

Cemeteries in the north and south of Cairo are called the City of the Dead. The tombs are not just gravestones. They are solid buildings with courtyards. They provide homes for over half a million people.

Poor people have lived in Cairo's cemeteries since the fifteenth century. More and more people move there every week.

The Egyptian government has accepted the cemeteries as a place where people live. They supply people with electricity and water.

▲ A man outside his cemetery home.

'There's no more peace and quiet here. Too many people moving in, you see, especially here in the tombs.' – Fatima, who lives in the City of the Dead.

21

'In the morning I go to school with my brother. In the afternoon we work for five or six hours. The money we make supports our family.' – Ahmed, a child worker.

▲ Ahmed works making mousetraps. He makes up to 100 a day.

CITY WORKERS

Jobs in Cairo are often low-paid and exhausting. Many poor people work long hours in hot, dirty workshops. Most of the goods they make are sold to tourists. Other people do 'odd jobs', such as shoe shining or minding cars.

Children in a workshop in Cairo. ▶

CHILD BEGGARS

Child beggars are a shocking but common sight in Cairo. Some have had a limb cut off so that people feel sorry for them and give them money. An older boy usually rules over the beggars. He takes part of their money in return for keeping other beggars away from their 'patch'.

'I am lucky. My brother got a job on a felucca and now I work for him. Before, I had to sell paper handkerchiefs and ask for money to survive.' – Mohammed, who used to be a beggar.

◄ Many young children have no chance of going to school.

INDUSTRY

In the city of Helwan, hi-tech machinery is used in the steelworks to make products that are sold all over the world.

Alexandria is a modern industrial city of over 3.7 million people. It is Egypt's most important port.

CAIRO BOAT PEOPLE

Many people in Cairo live on battered houseboats on the River Nile. Each boat is 3 to 6 metres long, with a plastic or canvas cover. Families of up to nine people are packed on to each boat. They earn money from tourists, and fish for food.

▲ Cairo boat people on the River Nile.

'We come from a village south of Cairo. We travel up the river to fish, and live here on the banks of the river with our families.' – Abdullah, a Cairo boat person.

COUNTRY LIFE

The countryside makes most of Egypt's wealth. But most farmers do not earn much money. They struggle to make a living from a small piece of land.

Most farmers grow crops, such as maize and vegetables, to feed their families. A cash crop such as sugar, oranges or bananas, is also grown to sell in the local market. Farmers have donkeys to pull ploughs and carry loads. Goats are kept for their meat and milk.

NUMBER OF FARM ANIMALS	
Buffaloes	3,150,000
Camels	135,000
Cows	3,022,000
Pigs	29,000
Sheep	4,300,000

'Farming is a good life if you own land. Children herd goats and cattle. Women work with men in the fields. For many, life has not changed since the time of the pharaohs.' – Mohammed, a villager in El Faiyûm Oasis.

A farmer looking at his crop. ▶

▲ A water pump driven by cattle.

IRRIGATION

The land in Egypt is so dry that 99 per cent of farmland has to be irrigated. Many canals and wells have been built to carry water from the Nile.

Most farmers use simple water pumps to bring up water. But many farmers now use diesel pumps, which pump the water faster.

Since the Aswân Dam was completed in 1970, the Nile waters have been controlled. There are no more floods or terrible droughts.

▲ Just one worker operates this modern milking parlour.

MODERN FARMS

There are huge farms, as well as small ones in Egypt. They are usually owned by the government and use hi-tech machinery. They grow cash crops, such as cotton, which are sold abroad to help pay off Egypt's debt.

MAIN CROPS GROWN IN EGYPT	
Summer:	Cotton, rice, maize
Winter:	Wheat, clover, beans
Summer and winter:	
	Fruit, potatoes and other vegetables

The government uses the money from its cash crops to import food such as wheat. It is cheaper to buy wheat from abroad than to grow it in Egypt.

TYPICAL COUNTRY HOUSE

Flat roof

Walls made from mud bricks

Windows without glass

Wooden shutters

DAILY LIFE

Daily life in the country-side is very simple. People either work on their own fields, or for other farmers. Some work on the large, modern farms. Women help in the fields as well as looking after their homes and children.

A farmer and his son returning from the market. ▼

FAMILIES

Many Egyptian farmers are poor. They have large families so their children can help on the farm. Often, their children do not go to school, although education would help them to break out of poverty.

Farm sizes in Egypt are getting smaller because when a farmer dies, the land is divided up among all the children.

▲ People come to the local souk, or market, to shop and chat to friends.

WOMEN'S DRESS

Nowadays in Egypt, Muslim women are expected to cover their bodies. They usually wear long dresses and headscarves. Some women wear the *negab*, which is a cloak that covers the whole body. Fatma, a young village woman, is happy to wear a huge scarf down to her waist that covers all but her face. But it is hard to work in a *negab*.

THE BEDOUIN

Bedouin people have always lived in the desert, herding sheep and goats. Now, many Bedouin move around for only part of the year. Some use cars or trucks to travel instead of camels. Many Bedouin are moving to the cities.

▲ Bedouin traders at a camel market. Camels are still used for carrying goods and people.

A Bedouin man with his camel. ▶

WHY IS EGYPT POOR?

▲ Egyptian farmers struggle to feed their large families.

Poverty is a huge problem in Egypt. Many families survive on very little money. They cannot rely on the government to help them. But why is Egypt so poor?

Since ancient times, Egypt has been ruled by different people. The British ruled Egypt from 1882 until its independence in 1922. They still had some control until 1952.

Britain did not want Egypt to grow richer. They wanted farmers to produce goods such as cotton for British factories. So the Egyptians were stopped from building their own factories.

EGYPT COMPARED TO RICHER COUNTRIES			
	EGYPT	BRITAIN	USA
POPULATION (millions)	68.47	58.83	278.357
LIFE EXPECTANCY (how long people expect to live)	67 years	77 years	77 years
ADULT LITERACY RATES (percentage of the the population who can read and write)	53.7%	99%	99%

Under British rule, Egyptian children were not allowed to go to university, so they could not become educated and help their country grow richer. This made it hard for Egypt to catch up with the industrial countries once it finally became independent.

President Nasser after the Suez Crisis. ▼

THE SUEZ CRISIS

The Suez Canal is the quickest route by sea from Europe to the Middle East. But it was owned by France and Britain, even after Egypt became independent.

In 1956, Egypt's President Nasser took control of the canal. Ship owners were to pay fees to go through the canal. Nasser wanted this money to pay for the building of the Aswân Dam.

Britain and France were furious. Together with Israel, they attacked Egypt. But the USA and the USSR made the attackers turn back. Nasser had won a fantastic victory.

▲ Egyptian soldiers at the Suez Canal during the crisis.

NATIONAL DEBT

Egypt cannot produce all the goods that it needs, so it has to buy goods from abroad. Also, Egypt has huge debts to other countries because it borrowed money for building the Aswân Dam, and for fighting wars against Israel in 1967 and 1973. This means that much of the money made from selling goods abroad goes straight back to the banks to pay off the debt.

EGYPT'S TRADE BALANCE

Egypt always has a trading loss because it has to buy in more goods than it sells. For example, if Egypt sells goods abroad worth £4 billion, but then buys £6 billion worth of goods, it will have a trade loss of £2 billion. Egypt then has to borrow more money, so it never manages to pay off its national debt.

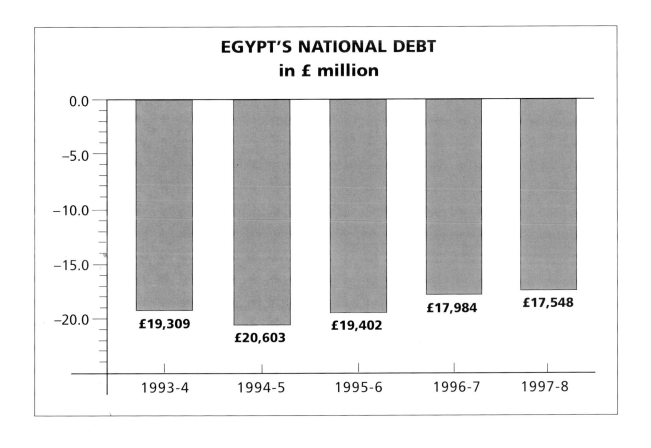

EGYPT'S NATIONAL DEBT
in £ million

1993-4	£19,309
1994-5	£20,603
1995-6	£19,402
1996-7	£17,984
1997-8	£17,548

ISLAMIC FUNDAMENTALISM

There is a struggle in Egypt between the Islamic fundamentalist movement and the government. The fundamentalists want strict Islamic laws, such as harsher punishments for crime, and a ban on alcohol. They carry out bombings and shootings to try to get their way.

In return, the government uses violence. Many Egyptians have been killed. The problems have badly affected business in Egypt.

ATTACKS ON TOURISTS

Money from tourists is very important to Egypt. Islamic fundamentalists sometimes attack tourists to try to get the government to listen to them. For example, in November 1997, 58 foreign tourists were murdered near Luxor. The government arrested fundamentalists and sentenced some to death. The violence means that fewer tourists want to visit Egypt.

◀ Islamic fundamentalists in prison.

THE BEDOUIN MAHALHA PEOPLE

The Bedouin Mahalha people used to live in the Gaza Strip, ruled by Israel. When Egypt took back the Sinai Desert from Israel in 1982, many Mahalha people were forced to leave Gaza, and lost their land.

Since then, a group of Mahalha people have lived in the Sinai Desert, near the border with Israel. Housed in rough shacks in a large camp, they have little hope of returning to Gaza.

Mahalha Bedouin in the Sinai Desert. ▶

EGYPT AND THE GULF WAR

In 1991, US-led forces freed Kuwait from control by Iraq. Egypt sent an armed force to help. In return, the USA took 7 billion dollars off Egypt's national debt.

DEVELOPMENT IN EGYPT

Egypt is a poor country, but it is trying to get richer through 'mega projects'. The projects aim to improve energy supplies, build new cities and improve farming.

OIL

Egypt has valuable oil supplies. Oil is used for energy in Egypt. It is also sold abroad. Sales of oil make up nearly half of Egypt's money from exports.

But oil supplies are running out. At the end of 1998, Egypt had only enough oil to last another 11.4 years. Also, since oil prices dropped in the 1980s, Egypt has made less money from sales.

TOURIST ATTRACTIONS

Since the tourist industry is so important to Egypt, new attractions such as the Aqua Park near Cairo have been built. Here, rich Egyptians and tourists enjoy the modern pools and huge water-slides.

▲ Aqua Park was built to attract tourists.

The Aswân Dam is over 3.5 kilometres wide. ▶

NATURAL GAS

Luckily, Egypt has natural gas as well as oil. Gas is used for energy in Egyptian homes. Egypt is planning to sell gas to other countries, too.

▲ Since the Aswân Dam was built, fishing in Lake Nasser has become an important industry.

OTHER ENERGY SOURCES

Surprisingly, for a country with so little rainfall, water is an important source of energy in Egypt. Hydroelectric power is made from the Aswân Dam.

Egypt is now building power stations that make electricity from wind and solar power.

A modern house in one of Egypt's new cities. ▶

NEW CITIES

Cairo, Alexandria and other Egyptian cities have become very overcrowded because so many people have moved there from the countryside. The Egyptian government wants to build new cities. Many have already been built. Others are being planned.

In 2000, nineteen new cities and towns were being built in Egypt. One city, 10th Ramadan, was built near Cairo. By 1999, over 900 factories had already opened there.

The air in the city of 10th Ramadan is cleaner than in Cairo and the houses are new. The Egyptian government want people to move out of Cairo to the new cities. But people find it hard to move to a different place to live.

▲ Flyovers have improved Cairo's roads.

IMPROVING CAIRO

Cairo is a busy, overcrowded and polluted city. To try and improve things, the government has built tall tower blocks for people to live in. The Cairo underground railway has helped to cut down the traffic jams.

A new sewage system has been built, with main sewage pipes bigger than a double-decker bus! Drinking water is now cleaner. But there are still half a million people living in poverty in the City of the Dead.

IMPROVING IMBABA

Imbaba is one of the poorest parts of Cairo. Since the mid-1990s, changes have been taking place here.

Imbaba used to be a slum with rubbish all over the streets. Few people had running water. Many children died from illnesses caused by the dirt. The death rate from disease was one of the highest in Cairo. But few doctors would work in the area.

Overcrowding in Imbaba was terrible. Over 600,000 people were packed into 2 square kilometres. People lived in half-built tower blocks or home-made mud and brick houses.

Finally, the government decided to do something. The main roads were paved. The tower blocks now have running water and sewers. The rubbish is collected regularly. There is a brand-new youth club. At last, things are getting better.

◄ Building work in Imbaba.

FARMING

Egypt has lots of people, but not much fertile land. Only 5.5 per cent of the land is used for people to live on.

The government wants much more land to be used. So there are 'mega projects' to irrigate and reclaim the desert so that it can be used for farming. This will mean that more people will be able to make a living from farming.

One problem with reclaimed land is that salt rises to the surface and kills the crops. ▶

◀ Dates can be grown on reclaimed land.

41

TH FUTUR

Egypt's government has big projects to develop cities, farming and industry. But the population is growing so fast that it is hard to help everyone. The government is encouraging people to have smaller families.

A health worker talking to women about birth control. ▼

'I work in a government clinic. Our job is to teach people about the need for population control, and the various ways this can be done.' – Sharira, health clinic worker in Luxor.

BIRTH CONTROL

The Egyptian Family Planning Association (EFPA) runs clinics where people can find out about birth control. It makes special efforts to work in the countryside, where the average family has five children.

The EFPA has had some success. The growth of Egypt's population has slowed down. In 1985 it was 2.2 per cent a year. In 1998 it was 1.9 per cent a year.

▲ Most women in the countryside cannot read, so this poster uses clear pictures about birth control.

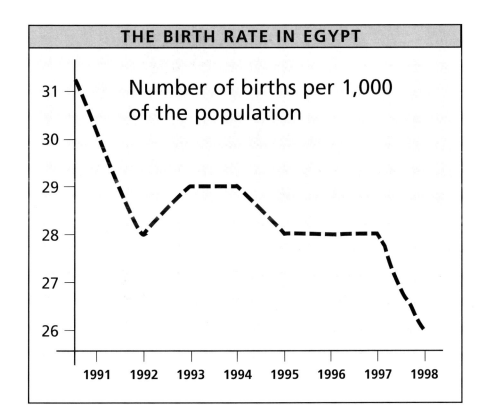

THE BIRTH RATE IN EGYPT

Number of births per 1,000 of the population

◄ As more people are taught about birth control, the birth rate has fallen.

▲ People earn low wages in Egypt, so hi-tech electronic goods can be made cheaply.

ECONOMY

The government wants the economy to grow so it can support the growing population. It has begun to sell businesses that it owns to private companies. It hopes that the new owners will make the businesses better and there will be more jobs. Also, hi-tech industries have been started.

The government is also looking at helping small businesses. Many people work in small businesses that are illegal because they do not pay tax. If the government helped them by giving them loans and grants, they would eventually do well and be able to pay tax.

Egypt has set up 'business parks', where factories have the latest technology. ▶

▲ Egyptian
people want
a better life.

Another government scheme is helping businesses to set up in areas away from the overcrowded Nile valley. They will provide work and encourage people to move to the new places.

Despite all these changes, most Egyptians still live in poverty. They do back-breaking work for long hours. It is up to the government to make sure that as Egypt gets richer, everyone can have a better life.

GLOSSARY

Astronomer A person who studies the Sun, Moon, planets and other objects in space.

Birth control Controlling the number of children you have.

Cash crop A crop that is grown to sell.

Crops Plants that are grown by people to use.

Debts Money borrowed that has to be paid back.

Delta A fan-shaped area of land where a river splits into many channels as it flows into the sea.

Drought A long time without rain, which causes damage to crops.

Economy The wealth and resources belonging to a country.

Exports Goods that are sold abroad.

Felucca A small boat with oars or sails.

Fertile Good for growing crops.

Flood plain The area on either side of a river where the river floods and dumps silt.

Fundamentalists People who keep very strictly to their religion.

Hydroelectric power Electricity made from the power of running water.

Impermeable Something that does not let gas, water or other liquid to pass through it.

Independence Free from foreign rule.

Irrigated Supplied with extra water, using pipes and canals, in order to grow crops.

Malaria A disease carried by mosquitoes. It can kill people.

Mosque A building where Muslims go to pray.

Natural resources Supplies of things from nature, such as water and oil, which can be used by people.

Oasis A place in the desert where water comes up from underground.

Plains Flat areas of land, without trees.

Population The people living in a place or country.

Porous Something that lets a liquid or gas pass through it.

Reclaim To take back.

Silt Tiny pieces of earth, sand, clay or rock carried by moving water.

Source The place where a river begins.

Tax Money that people have to pay to the government.

TOPIC WEB

Science
Ecosystems and conservation
Habitats: deserts – adaptation of plants and animals
Energy: HEP from Aswân Dam

History
Colonial rule
The break-up of European empires
Nasser and the Suez Crisis

Geography
Comparison of urban with rural life
Farming
Irrigation
Population and settlements
Rivers and floods: the Nile and the Aswân Dam
Weather and climate: khamsin

EGYPT

Religion
Islam
Mosques and worship
The position of women in Islam

English and Literacy
Egyptian myths and legends
Debate: should Egyptians have fewer children?
Read and write poems about life by a river
Role play: life as a Cairo boat person

ICT
Use websites to find out up-to-date information about Egypt
Collate climate statistics about a place in Egypt and make a weather database
Use ICT resources to make a presentation about an aspect of the book

Music and Art
Egyptian musical instruments and traditions
The River Nile as a theme for painting and collage

FINDING OUT MORE

BOOKS TO READ
Country Fact Files: Egypt by Emma Loveridge (Hodder Wayland, 1999)

Look what came from Egypt by Miles Harvey (Cherrytree, 1999)

Postcards from Egypt by Helen Arnold (Zöe Books, 1996)

TEACHING PACKS
Oxfam has a video pack: *Cairo: Four children and their city*, and a teaching pack with photos: *The Thread of the Nile*.

ADDRESSES AND WEBSITES
Department for International Development
94 Victoria St, London SW1E 5JL
Website: www.dfid.gov.uk

Egyptian State Information Service
Website: www.us.sis.gov.eg
Government information and statistics about all aspects of Egyptian life.

Oxfam, 274 Banbury Rd, Oxford OX2 7DZ
Website: www.oxfam.org.uk/coolplanet has resources for children and teachers.

UNICEF, 55 Lincoln's Inn Fields, London WC2A 3NB
Website: www.unicef.org.uk
Resources for schools about people in other lands.

INDEX